Ready-to-Use Sermon Outlines

Russell E. Spray

Copyright 1986 by
Baker Book House Company

ISBN: 0-8010-8268-4

Printed in the United States of America

Scripture references are taken from the
King James Version of the Holy Bible.

Ready-to-Use Sermon Outlines

Contents

Foreword 7

1. How to Beat Discouragement 8
   Psalm 42:5
2. How Christians Should Speak 10
   Psalm 26:7
3. How to Get Your Prayers Answered 12
   James 5:16
4. How to Feel God's Peace 14
   Philippians 4:7
5. How Jesus Cares 16
   1 Peter 5:7
6. How to S-H-A-R-E Christ 18
   Mark 16:15
7. Jesus Our L-O-R-D 20
   1 Timothy 6:15
8. L-I-F-T Up Christ 22
   John 12:32
9. P-A-T-I-E-N-C-E 24
   Luke 21:19
10. Praise the Lord 26
    Psalm 113:3
11. Practice the Truth 28
    John 14:6
12. Present Yourself to God 30
    Romans 12:1
13. S-A-F-E in Christ 32
    John 14:1
14. Something New Is Needed 34
    Isaiah 43:19

15. Tactics Satan Uses   36
    1 Peter 5:8
16. Take T-I-M-E for Christ   38
    Romans 13:11
17. The P-A-T-H of the Just   40
    Proverbs 4:18
18. The Bread of L-I-F-E   42
    John 6:35
19. The Christian's Admonition   44
    1 Corinthians 15:58
20. The God of Hope   46
    Psalm 42:5
21. The Holy Spirit in Believers   48
    John 14:17
22. The Magnificent Christ   50
    Matthew 28:18
23. The Never-Changing God   52
    Malachi 3:6
24. The "Now" Generation   54
    Matthew 6:33
25. The T-R-U-E God   56
    1 John 5:20
26. Win over Sin, Self, Satan   58
    Philippians 4:13
27. You Can Overcome   60
    John 16:33
28. Your Potential Through Christ   62
    Philippians 4:13

Foreword

These ready-to-use sermon outlines are just that: ready to use. Designed for busy ministers, they speak simply, sincerely, sensibly and scripturally.

My prayer is that all who use these outlines and hear the sermons they produce will be abundantly blessed and that God will be glorified.

Russell E. Spray

1

How to Beat Discouragement

"Why art thou cast down, O my soul? and why art thou disquieted in me? hope thou in God: for I shall yet praise him . . ." (Ps. 42:5).

Perhaps above all else, Satan tries to defeat God's people through discouragement. The following admonitions will help us win over discouragement.

I. Prove the Promises of God
"For all the promises of God in him are yea, and in him Amen . . ." (2 Cor. 1:20).
  A. Many Christians don't experience God's benevolence in their lives because they fail to appropriate his promises concerning their personal needs.
  B. We must realize that God's promises apply to our every need. We must read them, remember them, and claim them as our own. Ps. 119:11

II. Practice the Presence of God
". . . lo, I am with you alway, even unto the end of the world" (Matt. 28:20).
  A. Facts and faith are more important than feelings. Although we do not always sense the presence of God, the fact remains that he is always with us. Heb. 13:5
  B. We must practice praising God and believing that he is there even when we do not feel his presence. To do so triggers our faith and brings God closer.

III. Pursue the Peace of God
". . . seek peace, and pursue it" (Ps. 34:14).
  A. Many times Christians fail to appropriate God's peace because they do not feel it.
  B. God's people must recognize that his peace is available to

them at all times. If we practice his will, we can enjoy the peace "which passeth all understanding" (Phil. 4:7).

IV. Proclaim the Power of God
". . . All power is given unto me in heaven and in earth" (Matt. 28:18).
   A. Millions of people talk about horsepower, steam power, and atomic power, but they fail to exalt God's power.
   B. Let us proclaim God's power. It transcends all man-made power. Paul declares, "I can do all things through Christ which strengtheneth me" (Phil. 4:13).

2

How Christians Should Speak

"That I may publish with the voice of thanksgiving, and tell of all thy wondrous works" (Ps. 26:7).

Does the speech of Christians stand out? The following points show us how Christians ought to speak.

I. Speak with Christ
   ". . . and truly our fellowship is with the Father, and with his Son Jesus Christ" (1 John 1:3).
   A. When they pray, many Christians do most of the talking. True prayer is two-way communication, a means of enjoying fellowship with God. 1 Cor. 1:9
   B. God's Word says that we are to "be still, and know that I am God" (Ps. 46:10). To be effective Christians we must not only speak to God but we must also listen while he speaks to us.
   C. Our prayers should include praise as well as petition. Ps. 113:1–3

II. Speak Like Christ
   "And be ye kind one to another . . ." (Eph. 4:32).
   A. Too many Christians forget that they must reflect Christ's love, especially where their manner of speech is concerned. Their conversations may be interspersed with unkind, rude, or obscene remarks. Eph. 4:31
   B. Christ spoke with kindness, understanding, and purity. He was not caught up in the careless vernacular of his day.
   C. We must strive to speak and act like Christ.

III. Speak About Christ
   ". . . talk ye of all his wondrous works" (Ps. 105:2).
   A. Many Christians talk about the weather, jobs, houses, cars—everything except the Lord.

B. Christians should enjoy talking about spiritual things because it enhances their fellowship both with God and their fellow Christians.
C. We should speak about Christ's saving power whenever an opportunity arises—at home, school, work, and play. Ps. 26:7

IV. Speak Through Christ
"For it is not ye that speak, but the Spirit of your Father which speaketh in you" (Matt. 10:20).
A. When we speak through Christ, he speaks through us.
B. To be effective, we must depend on the Lord and speak through his strength and power, not relying on ourselves.
C. We should believe that Christ is saying the right words to the right people at the right time and place through us. Ps. 119:27

3

How to Get Your Prayers Answered

". . . The effectual fervent prayer of a righteous man availeth much" (James 5:16).

Many Christians pray to God but have difficulty hearing his answer. The following suggestions may help believers discern God's responses to their prayers.

I. Be Personal in Prayer
". . . but in every thing by prayer . . . let your requests be made known unto God" (Phil. 4:6).
- A. Many people don't have focus in their prayers. They may pray about many things in general, yet about nothing in particular. Their prayers accomplish little.
- B. We must be specific in our prayers. God is our Father; we are his children. We should talk to him openly and freely about people, problems, and circumstances. Ps. 37:40

II. Be Positive in Prayer
"Seven times a day do I praise thee because of thy righteous judgments" (Ps. 119:164).
- A. Many Christians are negative when they pray. They tell God about all the bad things and forget to thank him for the good things.
- B. We must be positive in prayer. We should spend at least as much time praising the Lord as we spend petitioning him. Eph. 5:20

III. Be Patient in Prayer
"I waited patiently for the LORD; and he . . . heard my cry" (Ps. 40:1).

A. Some Christians get impatient if their prayers are not answered on demand.
B. We must be patient in prayer and trust God's time and method. He knows best how and when to answer. Ps. 27:14

IV. Be Persistent in Prayer

". . . men ought always to pray, and not to faint" (Luke 18:1)

A. Many Christians fail to persist in prayer as they should. They give up too easily. They quit if they do not get an answer the first time they ask for one.
B. We must keep on keeping on. We must never give up. Be personal, positive, patient, and persistent, and God will answer your prayers. Ps. 37:5

4

How to Feel God's Peace

"And the peace of God, which passeth all understanding, shall keep your hearts and minds through Christ Jesus" (Phil. 4:7).

Christians can feel God's peace by practicing the following admonitions.

I. Prayer
   ". . . but in every thing by prayer . . ." (Phil. 4:6).
   A. Many Christians readily pray about the big challenges that come in life, but they are reluctant about taking the little things to God in prayer.
   B. God desires that we bring everything to him in prayer. This includes the good and bad, the great and small. To receive God's peace, we must surrender all.
   C. We must also be patient and pray repeatedly for God's will. Persistence pays off, so keep on asking, seeking, and knocking. Matt. 7:7–8

II. Petition
   ". . . and supplications . . ." (Phil. 4:6).
   A. Some Christians demand things from God, grieving him with their commands. Such prayers are ineffective.
   B. We must come to God in humble supplication, petitioning him for our needs and desires.
   C. God gives peace to those who come to him in loving submission. 1 Peter 5:6

III. Praise
   ". . . with thanksgiving . . ." (Phil. 4:6).
   A. Although many Christians petition the Lord repeatedly for their needs, they fail to praise him as they should for answers to their prayers.

B. Praising the Lord is a must if we are to receive his continued blessings and peace.
C. God is worthy of all our praise. We can never offer adequate praise to him. The psalmist said, "his praise shall continually be in my mouth" (Ps. 34:1).

5

How Jesus Cares

"Casting all your care upon him; for he careth for you" (1 Peter 5:7).

One thing is certain: Jesus Christ cares for us. What are some of the ways he expresses his love and concern?

I. Jesus Dares
". . . that he by the grace of God should taste death for every man" (Heb. 2:9).
  A. Many people resist getting involved. They go to great lengths to avoid any involvements which might cost them time and effort.
  B. Jesus dared to get involved. At Calvary he became our atonement for sin, paying the debt for us by giving his own life. 1 Cor. 15:3
  C. Jesus is actively involved today. He cares about everything that concerns his people. We must also dare to get involved in the needs of others.

II. Jesus Shares
"And that he died for all, that they which live should not henceforth live unto themselves . . ." (2 Cor. 5:15).
  A. Selfish people are tightfisted with God and others. They try to keep their blessings all to themselves.
  B. Jesus shares his riches with all who come to him in faith. He is ready to forgive the penitent and lift the fallen. He cares. Rom. 8:17
  C. We must also share with others. A smile, a kind word, or a helping hand can reveal Christ to the lost and unhappy.

III. Jesus Spares
"Who gave himself a ransom for all, to be testified in due time" (1 Tim. 2:6).

A. Because of sin, mankind was under the penalty of death. Jesus became our substitute. Refusing to spare himself, he gave his life for us, suffering in our place. 1 Thess. 5:10.
B. Because he did not spare himself, Jesus spares his people many woes and miseries. They do not have to suffer the penalty of sin.
C. We must also seek to spare others. Words of sympathy and understanding often cause resentments and strife to disappear.

IV. Jesus Bears

"For when we were yet without strength, in due time Christ died for the ungodly" (Rom. 5:6).

A. Many try unsuccessfully to carry their own burdens. Jesus bore our sins on the cross at Calvary. When we forsake our sins and trust him, we are set free. John 8:36
B. We must lighten the burdens of others by pointing them to the One who is able to carry their load.
C. Jesus cares—he dares, he shares, he spares, and he bears. Rom. 8:34–39

6

How to S-H-A-R-E Christ

"And he said unto them, Go ye into all the world, and preach the gospel to every creature" (Mark 16:15).

Here are some ways that Christians can share Christ.

I. S-peak for Christ
   "For it is not ye that speak, but the Spirit of your Father which speaketh in you" (Matt. 10:20).
   A. Many people are hesitant or embarrassed to speak out for Christ. They fear rejection or humiliation.
   B. If we are to share Christ, we must be willing to speak for him. He will give us the right words to say and arrange the proper time and place in which we are to say them. Eph. 4:15

II. H-old to Christ
   "Let us hold fast the profession of our faith without wavering; (for he is faithful that promised)" (Heb. 10:23).
   A. The faith of many Christians wavers. They fail to pray, read God's Word, and attend church regularly.
   B. If we are to share Christ, we must stay close to him ourselves. We must be diligent in our fellowship with him, renewing our faith daily. James 4:8

III. A-dvance with Christ
   "I can do all things through Christ which strengtheneth me" (Phil. 4:13).
   A. Many Christians become discouraged and lose enthusiasm. They fail to make progress in their walk with Christ.
   B. We must advance with Christ if we are to share him. We must not retreat or stand still. He will supply the strength we need to go forward. Eph. 3:16

IV. R-ejoice in Christ
"Rejoice in the Lord alway: and again I say, Rejoice" (Phil. 4:4).
   A. Some Christians fail to share because they do not rejoice in the Lord as much as they should. Their outlook is negative.
   B. People are looking for happiness. If they see it in us, they will respond. They will seek out the joy that we radiate. Gal. 5:22–23

V. E-ndure Through Christ
"Looking unto Jesus the author and finisher of our faith; who . . . endured the cross . . ." (Heb. 12:2).
   A. Jesus endured the cross for us. Therefore, we can endure through the strength he gives us.
   B. Share Christ—speak for him, hold to him, advance with him, rejoice in him, and endure through him. Matt. 24:13

7

Jesus Our L-O-R-D

". . . who is the blessed and only Potentate, the King of kings, and Lord of lords" (1 Tim. 6:15).

To be a Christian is to be Christlike. Let us emulate the following attributes of Jesus our Lord.

I. L-oving Jesus
". . . the Son of God, who loved me, and gave himself for me" (Gal. 2:20).
  A. Many are lax when it comes to loving their fellowman. They hold resentments, failing to forgive as they should.
  B. Jesus is loving and forgiving. He forgives the vilest sinner and loves the most unlovable. He accepts all who come to him in faith. We must also love others. John 15:17

II. O-bliging Jesus
". . . for his great love wherewith he loved us . . . in his kindness toward us through Christ Jesus" (Eph. 2:4–7).
  A. Many Christians are self-centered. They are possessive of the blessings granted them.
  B. Jesus was obliging—self-giving. He gave himself. We must give more of ourselves as Jesus did. John 10:10–11

III. R-eliable Jesus
"Let us hold fast the profession of our faith . . . (for he is faithful that promised)" (Heb. 10:23).
  A. Many people are undependable. They are careless when it comes to keeping promises.
  B. Jesus never fails to keep his word; he always makes good his promises. We must strive to be reliable too. 2 Cor. 1:20

IV. D-ivine Jesus

". . . This is my beloved Son, in whom I am well pleased" (Matt. 3:17).

A. Jesus was human, but also divine. He lived humbly and died on the cross, but arose victorious over death, hell, and the grave.
B. Because Jesus lives, we can live also. Those who repent and believe become alive in Christ. Christians will live eternally with the Lord. John 14:19

8

L-I-F-T Up Christ

"And I, if I be lifted up from the earth, will draw all men unto me" (John 12:32).

The following points are some ways we can honor and exalt Christ.

I. L-ove Him
   ". . . Thou shalt love the Lord thy God with all thy heart . . . soul . . . strength . . . mind . . ." (Luke 10:27).
   A. Many people love possessions, pleasure, and position more than the Lord. They follow selfish pursuits instead of seeking to please God.
   B. To love Christ as we should, we must surrender everything to him. We must give him first place in our lives, totally committing our entire selves to him. Matt. 6:33

II. I-mitate Him
   "For I have given you an example, that ye should do as I have done to you" (John 13:15).
   A. Pride, no doubt, is the most prevalent sin of our day. Jesus gave us an example of humility. We are to follow in his steps. 1 Peter 2:21
   B. We imitate the Lord by assisting the less fortunate, having compassion on the suffering, comforting the lonely, and sharing Christ with the lost as opportunity arises. James 4:10

III. F-ollow Him
   ". . . If any man will come after me, let him deny himself, and take up his cross, and follow me" (Matt. 16:24).
   A. Many are willing to follow Christ as long as he leads where they want to go. They seek ease and pleasure.

B. If we are to lift up Christ, we must be ready to follow him everywhere, even into the valley of sorrow and suffering if that is where he leads. He is with us and has promised never to leave us nor forsake us. If we tread in Christ's steps, the final destination will bring only blessings and eternal happiness. Heb. 13:5; 1 Peter 2:21

IV. T-riumph in Him

"But thanks be to God, which giveth us the victory through our Lord Jesus Christ" (1 Cor. 15:57).

A. Many Christians lack victory because they fail to give thanks and praise the Lord enough.

B. The psalmist said, "Blessed be the name of the LORD from this time forth and for evermore" (Ps. 113:2). To be triumphant, we must lift up Christ with praise.

9

P-A-T-I-E-N-C-E

"In your patience possess ye your souls" (Luke 21:19).

Patience is a necessary virtue in the life of Christians. God uses it to help them mature spiritually.

I. P-erfects
". . . the trying of your faith worketh patience. But let patience have her perfect work . . ." (James 1:3–4).
A. Patience perfects God's children.
B. We must hold fast during difficult times.

II. A-ccepts
"Wait on the LORD: be of good courage . . ." (Ps. 27:14).
A. Patience means that we accept whatever God allows to happen.
B. Patience does not necessarily mean that we like all that God allows, but it holds us steady in difficult times.

III. T-eaches
". . . knowing that tribulation worketh patience; And patience, experience; and experience, hope" (Rom. 5:3–4).
A. We are told that experience is the best teacher.
B. Patience brings experience, thus teaching us how to please God.

IV. I-nspires
". . . and let us run with patience the race that is set before us" (Heb. 12:1).
A. A runner is inspired to reach the goal that is set for him.
B. We must run life's race with patience.

V. E-levates
"For ye have need of patience, that . . . ye might receive the promise" (Heb. 10:36).

A. It takes time for God to answer some prayers, but he always responds with what is best for his children.
B. Patience lifts us from despair and gives us hope.

VI. N-urtures

"... *the husbandman waiteth for the precious fruit of the earth, and hath long patience for it ...*" *(James 5:7).*

A. It takes time for a beautiful rose to bloom or for an oak tree to grow to a stalwart height.
B. We must be patient in our quest for spiritual maturity.

VII. C-onquers

"Strengthened with all might, according to his glorious power, unto all patience and longsuffering with joyfulness" (Col. 1:11).

A. Joshua patiently circled Jericho day after day knowing that his faith in God's power would bring him victory.
B. We can also conquer through faith and patience.

VIII. E-ndures

"For when God made promise to Abraham ... Saying, Surely blessing I will bless thee, and multiplying I will multiply thee. And so, after he had patiently endured, he obtained the promise" (Heb. 6:13–15).

A. Abraham had to put aside doubts and endure many childless years before God fulfilled his covenant.
B. As good soldiers of Jesus Christ, we must patiently endure until the end.

10

Praise the Lord

"From the rising of the sun unto the going down of the same, the LORD's name is to be praised" (Ps. 113:3).

Many Christians fail to praise the Lord enough. He is worthy of our tribute and we should praise him continuously.

I. Praise Him for Salvation
   "Thanks be unto God for his unspeakable gift" (2 Cor. 9:15).
   A. Christ is God's unspeakable gift. He gave his only begotten Son to die for our sins because he loved us so much. John 3:16
   B. Christ gave himself to bring salvation to a lost world. We must praise him for our salvation. We will never be able to thank him adequately for his great sacrifice.

II. Praise Him for Serenity
   "And the peace of God, which passeth all understanding, shall keep your hearts and minds through Christ Jesus" (Phil. 4:7).
   A. Many people take the peace of God for granted.
   B. We should never fail to praise God for his peace—a peace "which passeth all understanding." God's peace keeps not only our hearts but our minds from distress and despair. Phil. 4:7

III. Praise Him for Sustenance
   "Who satisfieth thy mouth with good things . . ." (Ps. 103:5).
   A. Many Christians trust in self-effort and help from other people instead of depending on God.
   B. All our blessings come from God. Recognizing this, we should praise him wholeheartedly. "Giving thanks always for all things unto God . . ." (Eph. 5:20).

IV. Praise Him for Security

"Fear thou not; for I am with thee: be not dismayed; for I am thy God . . ." (Isa. 41:10).

A. Insecurity abounds in today's world. There is no safe place outside of Christ.
B. Christians do not have to be afraid for God is with them. We should praise him because our future is safe in Christ. John 14:1–3

11

Practice the Truth

"Jesus saith unto him, I am the way, the truth, and the life: no man cometh unto the Father, but by me" (John 14:6).

The following points expound ways to practice the truth.

I. Think the Truth
". . . whatsoever things are true, whatsoever things are honest . . . think on these things" (Phil. 4:8).
- A. Christians are subject to worldly thoughts, but need not dwell on them.
- B. We should replace evil thoughts with good ones, dishonest thoughts with truthful ones.

II. See the Truth
". . . the Spirit of truth . . . will guide you into all truth . . . and he will shew you things to come" (John 16:13).
- A. Because of television, many people live in an unreal world. They believe the fantasies fed to them instead of the truth.
- B. We must look to Christ and his Word. He is the source of all truth.

III. Hear the Truth
". . . O God . . . hear me, in the truth of thy salvation" (Ps. 69:13).
- A. The voices of radio and television have hypnotized the minds of millions.
- B. We must listen to the voice of Jesus, the Truth, although he often speaks in only a whisper.

IV. Speak the Truth
"But speaking the truth in love, may grow up into him in all things . . ." (Eph. 4:15).

A. Speaking the truth must become a habit. Some people become careless about being completely honest.
B. We cannot win others through harsh, unkind words. We can only win them by speaking "the truth in love."

V. Do the Truth

". . . let us not love in word, neither in tongue; but in deed and in truth" (1 John 3:18).

A. Some people may tell the truth but their actions deny their words.
B. Let us practice doing the truth. We are told that actions speak louder than words.

VI. Walk in Truth

"I have no greater joy than to hear that my children walk in truth" (3 John 4).

A. Our daily walk is important. God has commanded that we walk in truth and love.
B. To walk in truth, we must think the truth, see the truth, hear the truth, speak the truth, and do the truth. 2 John 1–4

12

Present Yourself to God

"I beseech you therefore, brethren, by the mercies of God, that ye present your bodies a living sacrifice, holy, acceptable unto God, which is your reasonable service" (Rom. 12:1).

Christians need to surrender themselves and submit to God without reserve.

I. Present Your Mind
"Let this mind be in you, which was also in Christ Jesus" (Phil. 2:5).
- A. Many Christians feel defeated because they dwell on negatives.
- B. With conscious deliberation, we must replace negative thoughts with positive ones.

II. Present Your Eyes
"But mine eyes are unto thee, O God the LORD . . ." (Ps. 141:8).
- A. Some Christians look at the sin in the world and in the church and center their attention on it.
- B. To be victorious, we must search for the good instead of the disagreeable. God has supplied many blessings which we can always find.

III. Present Your Ears
"I will hear what God . . . will speak . . ." (Ps. 85:8).
- A. Millions of people listen to the filth and smut that come over the airways.
- B. We must keep our ears tuned to God and his Word. We should listen to the good message that he has for us.

IV. Present Your Tongue

"And be ye kind one to another . . ." (Eph. 4:32).

A. Some Christians are careless in their conversations. They are inconsiderate of others.
B. God can enable us to speak the right words to the right people at the right times.

V. Present Your Hands

". . . I will shew thee my faith by my works" (James 2:18).

A. Many Christians work diligently at selfish pursuits but are lax about doing God's work.
B. We must be ready to lift, encourage, comfort, and witness for the Lord.

VI. Present Your Feet

"As ye have therefore received Christ Jesus the Lord, so walk ye in him" (Col. 2:6).

A. People are on the go. Ours is a mobile society.
B. Christians must go for the Lord. The Holy Spirit will direct the steps of those who yield themselves to him. John 16:13

13

S-A-F-E in Christ

"Let not your heart be troubled: ye believe in God, believe also in me" (John 14:1).

No person is safe outside of Christ. In Christ we are:

I. S-ecure
"But my God shall supply all your need according to his riches in glory by Christ Jesus" (Phil. 4:19).
A. Millions of people are insecure. There is no true security outside of Jesus Christ in today's competitive world.
B. Christians should not falter in their confidence because their security lies in Christ. He cannot fail. Security is not found in possessions but in being possessed by Christ. John 14:13–14

II. A-ctive
"With good will doing service, as to the Lord, and not to men" (Eph. 6:7).
A. Some Christians exert energy only in the pursuit of personal interests. They are lax when it comes to serving God.
B. There are many ways to be active for God. Give a smile, a kind word, a warm handshake. When we help others, God will also reward us with good. Eph. 6:8

III. F-ree
"If the Son therefore shall make you free, ye shall be free indeed" (John 8:36).
A. Many Christians are held in bondage by the world and their own selfish pursuits. They fail to glorify God and be the blessings they could be.

B. Jesus is the truth that sets us free. He said, "And ye shall know the truth, and the truth shall make you free" (John 8:32).

IV. E-nduring
"But he that shall endure unto the end, the same shall be saved" (Matt. 24:13).
A. Christians who hope to get to heaven on flowery beds of ease may be unable to endure when circumstances become rough.
B. We must be prepared to withstand trial, trouble, and testing as good soldiers of Jesus Christ. He will enable those who trust in him to endure. 2 Tim. 2:3

14

Something New Is Needed

"Behold, I will do a new thing; now it shall spring forth; shall ye not know it? (Isa. 43:19).

Christians should review and renew their standing in Christ.

I. New Hope
". . . hope thou in God: for I shall yet praise him for the help of his countenance" (Ps. 42:5).
- A. Many people are hopeful about temporal things. Their values lie in money, cars, houses, and land. They are doomed to disappointment.
- B. We must put our hope in the Lord God. Earthly possessions will eventually be gone, but God's spiritual blessings never decrease in value and are everlasting.
- C. When all else comes to naught, God offers new hope. "Hope in God" (Ps. 43:5).

II. New Faith
". . . Have faith in God" (Mark 11:22).
- A. The apostles asked the Lord to increase their faith. Many Christians fail to increase in faith. Therefore, they become stagnant. Luke 17:5
- B. Our faith must be exercised and renewed with daily use. When we work our faith, our faith works for us.
- C. New faith can be ours for the asking. 1 John 5:4

III. New Love
"By this we know that we love the children of God, when we love God . . ." (1 John 5:2).

A. The love of many Christians has grown cold. The Lord wants us to be more like him, to cause us to "increase and abound in love" (1 Thess. 3:12).
B. New hope, new faith, new love—these three qualities are vital to the Christian life.
C. Something new is needed. Everyone needs to be revived occasionally. God offers us fresh hope, a stronger faith, a greater love. Let us be renewed in him today.

15

Tactics Satan Uses

"Be sober, be vigilant; because your adversary the devil, as a roaring lion, walketh about, seeking whom he may devour" (1 Peter 5:8).

Satan uses various ways to defeat God's people.

I. He Amuses
". . . Satan, which deceiveth the whole world . . ." (Rev. 12:9).
A. We live in a pleasure-oriented society. Millions of people are searching for entertainment.
B. Satan takes advantage of man's desire for amusement. He sometimes blurs a Christian's perception of what is right and wrong. We must "try the spirits whether they are of God" (1 John 4:1).

II. He Excuses
"And the devil that deceived them . . ." (Rev. 20:10).
A. Many people can find alibis for neglecting God's work. They easily excuse themselves from those things they should be doing.
B. Satan is ready to excuse every evil word, thought, deed, and action. We must be constantly aware of his tactics and refuse to succumb to the temptations which he presents. Gen. 3:1–7

III. He Confuses
". . . Satan hath desired to have you . . ." (Luke 22:31).
A. Satan confuses Christians by causing them to question God's Word, work, will, and way.
B. Christians must be grounded in the faith and in God's Word. We must heed God's admonitions and claim his promise to "stablish, strengthen, settle you" (1 Peter 5:10).

IV. He Accuses
". . . the accuser of our brethren . . ." (Rev. 12:10).
A. After Satan has amused, excused, and confused the Christian, he then accuses him of wrongdoing.
B. Satan is called "the accuser of our brethren." "And they overcame him by the blood of the Lamb, and by the word of their testimony . . ." (Rev. 12:10–11).

16

Take T-I-M-E for Christ

"And that, knowing the time, that now it is high time to awake out of sleep: for now is our salvation nearer than when we believed" (Rom. 13:11).

Millions of people are caught up in their personal pursuits. They take little or no time for Christ. Christians need to:

I. T-rust Him
"Trust in the LORD with all thine heart; and lean not unto thine own understanding" (Prov. 3:5).
  A. Many people put their trust in money. They depend on their earthly possessions more than on the Lord.
  B. Houses and land and silver and gold are fleeting. They do not endure. The Lord is eternal. He never fails. We must rely on him. Ps. 37:3

II. I-mitate Him
"For I have given you an example, that ye should do as I have done to you" (John 13:15).
  A. Some Christians do not try to follow the example that Christ set for them. They are snobbish and self-seeking. They fail to imitate Christ's humility and love.
  B. We, as Christians, should exemplify Christ through acts of kindness, understanding, and generosity. We reflect his loving nature by sharing with the needy and praying for the lost and hurting. 1 Peter 2:21

III. M-agnify Him
"O magnify the LORD with me, and let us exalt his name together" (Ps. 34:3).
  A. Many Christians do not sufficiently praise the Lord. They take their blessings for granted and fail to thank God for them.

B. We can never magnify the Lord enough; he is worthy of unlimited praise. The psalmist said, "His praise shall continually be in my mouth" (Ps. 34:1).

IV. E-xpect Him

"Watch therefore: for ye know not what hour your Lord doth come" (Matt. 24:42).

A. The Scriptures tell us that the coming of the Lord is imminent (Luke 21:28). Conditions in our world indicate this. The time is short and a lot remains to be done—personal preparation and outreach to others so that they, too, might be prepared.
B. We must take time for Christ. His return is imminent; soon we shall reign with him eternally. ". . . and so shall we ever be with the Lord" (1 Thess. 4:17).

17

The P-A-T-H of the Just

"But the path of the just is as the shining light, that shineth more and more unto the perfect day" (Prov. 4:18).

The Christian path leads heavenward to the perfect day. It is a:

I. Path of P-atience
"In your patience possess ye your souls" (Luke 21:19).
- A. Many Christians lack patience. Because of this deficiency, they fail to please God and also fail to be witnesses and outlets for God's saving power.
- B. Patience is necessary for successful Christian living. God sometimes allows troubles and trials to come in an effort to strengthen our faith and patience. "Knowing that tribulation worketh patience" (Rom. 5:3).

II. Path of A-ffection
"And walk in love, as Christ also hath loved us . . ." (Eph. 5:2).
- A. Most Christians can make progress on this path. We must love not only God and ourselves but we must also love other people. 1 John 4:21
- B. Making an effort to give a smile, a kind word, a warm handshake, or a helping hand increases our love. ". . . every one that loveth him that begat loveth him also that is begotten of him" (1 John 5:1).

III. Path of T-rust
"And the Lord shall help them, and deliver them . . . because they trust in him" (Ps. 37:40).
- A. Some Christians lack God's blessings because they fail to trust him as they should. They trust in money, jobs,

houses, and cars, things which leave them with only a false sense of security.
B. God deserves first place in our lives. He also deserves our ultimate trust. He never changes. He never fails. His promises are reliable. Ps. 37:3–5

IV. Path to H-eaven
"To an inheritance incorruptible . . . reserved in heaven for you" (1 Peter 1:4).
A. Many people act like they're going to take their earthly possessions with them into the next life. How foolish! Everything must be left behind.
B. The Christian path leads to heaven. We must lay up treasures there, "where neither moth nor rust doth corrupt, and where thieves do not break through nor steal" (Matt. 6:20).

18

The Bread of L-I-F-E

". . . I am the bread of life: he that cometh to me shall never hunger; and he that believeth on me shall never thirst" (John 6:35).

Bread has been called "the staff of life." Jesus, our spiritual bread, is the source of eternal life. He is:

I. L-iving Bread
"I am the living bread which came down from heaven . . ." (John 6:51).
  A. Earthly bread is limited in value. It cannot supply all the nutritional and physical needs of man. John 6:58
  B. Jesus is the living Bread. He forgives and sustains those who accept and partake of him. Jesus said, "Because I live, ye shall live also" (John 14:19).

II. I-nviting Bread
". . . every one which seeth the Son, and believeth on him, may have everlasting life . . ." (John 6:40).
  A. Freshly-baked bread is inviting. Its tantalizing aroma arouses appetites.
  B. Jesus, the Bread of Life, appeals to the longing of the heart and soul. His invitation is extended to every individual in the world. Ps. 34:8

III. F-illing Bread
". . . I am the bread of life: he that cometh to me shall never hunger . . ." (John 6:35).
  A. Homemade bread is filling and satisfying. Nutrients must be added to commercial bread to give it substance.
  B. Jesus, the Bread of Life, is satisfying and sustaining. He fills the Christian's life with love and the promise of eternal life. His blessings come to those who "hunger and thirst after righteousness: for they shall be filled" (Matt. 5:6).

IV. E-nduring Bread
". . . if any man eat of this bread, he shall live for ever . . ." (John 6:51).
   A. Earthly bread does not sustain man for very long. Its nutritional value is short-lived at best; it must be eaten continuously.
   B. Jesus, the Bread of Life, sustains eternally. When we accept him as our Savior and Lord, we receive everlasting life. John 6:47–51

19

The Christian's Admonition

"Therefore, my beloved brethren, be ye stedfast, unmoveable, always abounding in the work of the Lord, forasmuch as ye know that your labour is not in vain in the Lord" (1 Cor. 15:58).

Christians are promised victory over death, but Paul also talks about how they should live while on earth.

I. Be Dependable
   ". . . be ye stedfast . . ." (1 Cor. 15:58).
   A. It is natural that Christians encounter some valleys in their spiritual walk. But it is important that during these low points they continue to seek God.
   B. God wants his people to be dependable—faithful in prayer, Bible study, and church attendance.
   C. A crown of life awaits the faithful. Rev. 2:10

II. Be Determined
   ". . . be . . . unmoveable . . ." (1 Cor. 15:58).
   A. When situations get rough, Christians sometimes lose sight of their source of strength—God, the Provider and Protector. They lack determination.
   B. As the apostle Paul admonished the Christians of his day, we must be "unmoveable" when it comes to serving the Lord.
   C. We must be determined to keep going regardless of the circumstances. Phil. 3:13–14

III. Be Diligent
   ". . . always abounding in the work of the Lord . . . " (1 Cor. 15:58).
   A. Too many Christians do not abound in the work of the Lord; they are slothful concerning their responsibilities to him.

B. Some are diligent when it comes to working for themselves or others, but fall short when it comes to doing God's work.
C. We must give God first place in our lives, "being fruitful in every good work" (Col. 1:10).

IV. Be Delighted

"... forasmuch as ye know that your labour is not in vain in the Lord" (1 Cor. 15:58).

A. Do God's work with a joyful attitude. Smile, encourage, and share Christ with delight.
B. Our desire should be to please God and to accomplish his will and work with joy.
C. Following Paul's admonition, we can say with the psalmist, "I delight to do thy will, O my God" (Ps. 40:8).

20

The God of Hope

". . . hope thou in God . . ." (Ps. 42:5).

The topic of hope is often neglected. The following points emphasize the necessity and value of hope.

I. "Hope"
   A. *"And now abideth faith, hope, charity [love], these three . . ." (1 Cor. 13:13).* Faith and love are necessary to the Christian life, but they can only be ignited by hope.
   B. Without hope, perseverance in Christ would be impossible. The Christian's hope is eternal life. "In hope of eternal life, which God, that cannot lie, promised before the world began" (Titus 1:2).

II. "Thou"
   A. Many people think of hope in the abstract. They fail to acknowledge that God is the source of hope. Ps. 119:116
   B. Hope, to be effective, must be personalized—"thou." We must know that God is within us and is helping us now. He also holds the future, which is bright with his promise.

III. "In"
   A. Hope must be "in" something or someone. Many put their hope in doctors, lawyers, or other people. Ultimately, they will be disappointed.
   B. Millions of people put their hope in temporal pursuits. They acquire homes, land, money, and influence, hoping that these will produce happiness and fulfillment. A person's hope must be placed securely in God. He alone is eternal and he alone can fulfill our needs and give us contentment. 1 Peter 1:21

IV. "God"
   A. People fail, promises fail, and pursuits fail. Everything and every person is subject to failure. Man inherited sin, mistakes, blunders, and failure from the Fall. God is the perfect Creator who remained unscathed; he is the only one who cannot fail.
   B. Our faith, our trust, and our hope must be in God. He promises, "I will be with thee: I will not fail thee, nor forsake thee" (Josh. 1:5).

21

The Holy Spirit in Believers

"Even the Spirit of truth; whom the world cannot receive, because it seeth him not, neither knoweth him: but ye know him; for he dwelleth with you, and shall be in you" (John 14:17).

It is God's wish that the Holy Spirit indwell Christians' hearts, enabling them to live victorious lives.

I. The Committing
"I beseech you therefore, brethren . . . that ye present your bodies a living sacrifice . . ." (Rom. 12:1).
- A. Some Christians commit a part of their lives to God but hold a portion in reserve for their selfish interests.
- B. Victory comes only through total commitment. We must surrender all we have to God without reserve. Prov. 3:5

II. The Cleansing
". . . purifying their hearts by faith" (Acts 15:9).
- A. Many Christians fall short of their spiritual potential in Christ because they fail to yield their hearts to God's cleansing power.
- B. When yielded Christians come to God in faith and obedience, they are cleansed and filled with the Holy Spirit. 1 John 1:7

III. The Comforting
". . . he shall give you another Comforter, that he may abide with you for ever" (John 14:16).
- A. When Jesus left his disciples, he promised that the Holy Spirit would come to them and be their Comforter.
- B. Even in a discomfortable world, the Holy Spirit is our source of comfort. We can rest in him. Ps. 37:7

IV. The Counseling
". . . he shall teach you all things, and bring all things to your remembrance . . ." (John 14:26).
A. There are many counselors today, but none can compare with the Holy Spirit. He surpasses them all in wisdom, guidance, and reassurance.
B. "Howbeit when he, the Spirit of truth, is come, he will guide you into all truth . . . and he will shew you things to come" (John 16:13).

V. The Conquering
"But ye shall receive power, after that the Holy Ghost is come upon you . . ." (Acts 1:8).
A. Nations try to conquer other nations. People try to conquer other people. Only Spirit-filled Christians can conquer sin.
B. The Holy Spirit brings conquering power to believers, enabling them to enjoy victory now and in the life to come. Phil. 4:13

22

The Magnificent Christ

"And Jesus came and spake unto them, saying, All power is given unto me in heaven and in earth" (Matt. 28:18).

If we are to be more like Christ, we need to know more about him.

I. His Masterful Life
   ". . . In the world ye shall have tribulation: but be of good cheer; I have overcome the world" (John 16:33).
   A. Many people spend their lives pursuing selfish interests. In the process, they are inconsiderate of other people; in the end they fail to achieve fulfillment in their own lives.
   B. Jesus had mastery over every situation. His was a selfless life. He calmed the angry sea, healed sicknesses, withstood persecution, and conquered death. He was in perfect harmony with his heavenly Father.
   C. We should strive to be more like Jesus. He is trustworthy, dependable, and always willing to help those in trouble. Phil. 4:13

II. His Merciful Lift
   "And Jesus, moved with compassion, put forth his hand, and touched him . . ." (Mark 1:41).
   A. Jesus felt compassion for those who were down but he also took action. Mark 1:31
   B. Christ spent much of his life on earth uplifting people. He helped the hungry by giving them food. He gave comfort to the bereaved, and forgiveness to sinners. Matt. 9:36
   C. We must care about others as Jesus did, depending on him to help us lift them up.

III. His Matchless Love
"And to know the love of Christ, which passeth knowledge . . ." (Eph. 3:19).
  A. Human love may fail. Mothers have been known to disown their children, but Jesus never forsakes his own.
  B. The love of Christ is so powerful that nothing can sever us from it. "Nor height, nor depth, nor any other creature, shall be able to separate us from the love of God, which is in Christ Jesus our Lord" (Rom. 8:39).
  C. Let us emulate the magnificent Christ—his masterful life, his merciful lift, and his matchless love.

23

The Never-Changing God

*"For I am the L*ORD*, I change not . . ."* *(Mal. 3:6).*

In the midst of an ever-changing world, it is comforting to know there are some things that do not change.

I. God's Promise Doesn't Change
"If my people . . . shall humble themselves, and pray . . . then will I . . . forgive their sin, and will heal their land" (2 Chron. 7:14).
   A. Many people make promises but fail to keep them because of a change of mind or circumstances.
   B. God's promise never fails. It is dependable—all who repent and believe will be saved.
   C. "Whereby are given unto us exceeding great and precious promises: that by these ye might be partakers of the divine nature . . ." (2 Peter 1:4).

II. God's Peace Doesn't Change
"And the peace of God . . . shall keep your hearts and minds through Christ Jesus" (Phil. 4:7).
   A. Millions are searching for peace. People think that they can find peace in friends, the latest fashions, and large bank accounts. Yet when a person acquires all this, he finds that peace still eludes him.
   B. Man's peace often fails, but God's peace is sure. It is given to those who heed his admonitions. Phil. 4:6
   C. The peace that is found in God is lasting and eternal. Heaven will be a place of peace, joy, and love.

III. God's Power Doesn't Change
". . . For there is no power but of God: the powers that be are ordained of God" (Rom. 13:1).
A. Mankind is striving for more power. Man's power is subject to change and failure.
B. God's power doesn't change. It brought the world into existence, and it is just as effective today.
C. God is waiting to lift and strengthen those who unreservedly trust him. "He giveth power to the faint; and to them that have no might he increaseth strength" (Isa. 40:29).

IV. God's Purpose Doesn't Change
"According to the eternal purpose which he purposed in Christ Jesus our Lord" (Eph. 3:11).
A. Man's purpose often falls by the side of the road in lieu of trouble or thwarted ambitions. God's purpose is eternal.
B. When man fell, God purposed in his love to save all who believe in him through Christ. John 3:16
C. God's promise, peace, power, and purpose never change. Jesus Christ is the same yesterday, today, and forever. Heb. 13:8

24

The "Now" Generation

"But seek ye first the kingdom of God, and his righteousness; and all these things shall be added unto you" (Matt. 6:33).

The "now" generation, in its impatience, can often make premature and detrimental demands.

I. Demands Pleasure Now
". . . ye may be glad also with exceeding joy" (1 Peter 4:13).
   A. We live in a pleasure-oriented world. Millions are seeking after pleasure and they want it now.
   B. We must be careful to seek after the will of God. It is his plan for our lives that will bring us lasting pleasure. Faithful worship, prayer, and fellowship with God's people bring pleasure in seeking his will.

II. Demands Possessions Now
"But lay up for yourselves treasures in heaven . . ." (Matt. 6:20).
   A. Ours is a materialistic society. Millions want their rewards now rather than working and waiting for them.
   B. We must give God first place, remembering that "the love of money is the root of all evil." We must be patient, work diligently, and give liberally.

III. Demands Popularity Now
"But seek ye first the kingdom of God . . . and all these things shall be added unto you" (Matt. 6:33).
   A. Some are unwilling to wait until friendship develops. They want instant acceptance, so they compromise their values. Their popularity is usually short-lived, only to be replaced by loneliness and guilt.

B. We must desire God's approval most of all. When we give him first place, working and witnessing for him, we will find solid friendships with others who share our love for God.

IV. Demands Promotion Now
"... *that he may exalt you in due time*" *(1 Peter 5:6)*.
A. Many demand instant promotion. They want an exalted position without earning it. If it comes, they are likely to find their success short-lived.
B. We must depend on God for promotion. We must be faithful to the tasks that are set before us and trust him for the results in his own time and way.

25

The T-R-U-E God

"And we know that the Son of God is come, and hath given us an understanding, that we may know him that is true, and we are in him that is true, even in his Son Jesus Christ. This is the true God, and eternal life" (1 John 5:20).

The following points help describe the T-R-U-E God.

I. T-rustworthy
"The Lord is not slack concerning his promise . . ." (2 Peter 3:9).
- A. Many Christians are undependable when it comes to spiritual commitment. They can be enthusiastic in their faith one moment, and feel spiritually dry the next. They are spiritually unstable.
- B. God always keeps his Word. He is trustworthy. ". . . there hath not failed one word of all his good promise . . ." (1 Kings 8:56).

II. R-edemptive
". . . not willing that any should perish, but that all should come to repentance" (2 Peter 3:9).
- A. Man cannot pull himself up by his own bootstraps. Without God, he is hopelessly lost.
- B. In Jesus Christ there is hope. God forgives and cleanses those who confess their sins, repent, and believe. 1 John 1:9

III. U-niversal
"For God so loved the world . . ." (John 3:16).
- A. God is not confined to a part of the world, a continent, or a nation. He is omnipresent and his love is universal.

B. Through Christ all the "whosoever wills" may be saved. Salvation is available to rich and poor, black and white, young and old alike. Acts 10:34

IV. E-ternal
"The eternal God is thy refuge, and underneath are the everlasting arms . . ." (Deut. 33:27).
- A. God doesn't endure for just a day, a week, month, or year. He is eternal. He is ready to help his children at all times according to his will.
- B. The true God is trustworthy, redemptive, universal, and eternal. ". . . This is the true God, and eternal life" (1 John 5:20).

26

Win over Sin, Self, Satan

"I can do all things through Christ which strengtheneth me" (Phil. 4:13).

It is only when we live in Christ that we can be assured of victory.

I. Salvation in Christ Denounces Sin
". . . the body of sin might be destroyed, that henceforth we should not serve sin" (Rom. 6:6).
  A. Many people profess to possess Christ as Savior and Lord, but they continue in their worldly way of life.
  B. Concerning the Christian, God's Word says: ". . . old things are passed away; behold, all things are become new" (2 Cor. 5:17).
  C. To win over sin, we must try to live true Christian lives. "In whom we have redemption through his blood, even the forgiveness of sins" (Col. 1:14).

II. Surrendering to Christ Dethrones Self
". . . present your bodies a living sacrifice, holy, acceptable unto God . . ." (Rom. 12:1).
  A. Many Christians fail to surrender all unreservedly to Christ. They hold something back for themselves.
  B. ". . . but yield yourselves unto God . . ." (Rom. 6:13). Victory is promised to those who surrender all to Christ.
  C. When Christians yield everything to Christ, the Holy Spirit cleanses and fills them with God's love. Self is dethroned.

III. Service for Christ Defeats Satan
"Comfort your hearts, and stablish you in every good word and work" (2 Thess. 2:17).

A. Satan is the Christian's adversary, but he is a defeated foe. We are more than conquerors through Christ. Rom. 8:37
B. Working for Christ defeats the devil. Give a smile, share a kind word, do a good deed, and seek to lead a lost soul to Jesus Christ. Col. 1:10
C. It is only through Christ that we can win over sin, self, and Satan. With the apostle Paul, "I can do all things through Christ which strengtheneth me" (Phil. 4:13).

27

You Can Overcome

"These things I have spoken unto you, that in me ye might have peace. In the world ye shall have tribulation: but be of good cheer; I have overcome the world" (John 16:33).

Too many Christians live defeated lives. The following points should help them turn defeat into victory.

I. Be Prayerful
". . . men ought always to pray, and not to faint" (Luke 18:1).
  A. Many Christians fail to pray sufficiently. They become easily discouraged and feel the situation is hopeless. They underestimate the power of communication with God.
  B. We must live our lives in a spirit of prayer. We should pray about the small things as well as the large ones. We can overcome anything through prayer. John 14:13–14

II. Be Patient
"In your patience, possess ye your souls" (Luke 21:19).
  A. Many Christians fall short when it comes to patience. Waiting can be difficult. Selfish motives encourage impatience, and that can lead to defeat.
  B. A lack of love also leads to impatience. The more love we possess, the more patience we receive. 1 Tim. 6:11

III. Be Positive
". . . whatsoever things are of good report . . . think on these things" (Phil. 4:8).
  A. Today's news is filled with reports of violence and crime in society; the media focuses on the negative aspects of life. The more shocking or destructive the event, the better news it promises to make.

B. We must look for the good not the bad in this world. To be "overcomers," we must dwell on things "of good report" (Phil. 4:8).

IV. Be Productive

". . . He that abideth in me, and I in him, the same bringeth forth much fruit . . ." (John 15:5).

A. Many live defeated lives because they devote so little of themselves to Christ. They are too busy with contemporary concerns.

B. We can overcome loneliness and spiritual unrest by helping the sick, lonely, and aged. We need to put ourselves out for the less fortunate. Deliberately denying ourselves to help others will produce spiritual fruit in our own lives. Witness to the lost as opportunities arise. Acts 1:8

28

Your Potential Through Christ

"I can do all things through Christ which strengtheneth me" (Phil. 4:13).

It is only through Christ that we can succeed. We falter and fail, but Christ's power is infinite and unfailing. Through Christ we have unlimited potential.

I. You Can Be in Christ
   "Therefore if any man be in Christ, he is a new creature . . ." (2 Cor. 5:17).
   A. The first step to spiritual success is the assurance of being "in Christ." Do you possess the joy of forgiveness? Are you free from guilt?
   B. Christians who yield themselves completely to God are cleansed and filled with his love.
   C. Totally committed Christians are "in Christ" and Christ is in them. He guides and directs their lives and empowers them for service. John 17:20–21

II. You Can Be for Christ
   ". . . Who is on the LORD's side? let him come unto me. . ." (Exod. 32:26).
   A. When the children of Israel made and worshiped a golden calf, Moses demanded that those who were on the Lord's side come out from among the others and take their stand for God.
   B. Today's Christians are deluged with evil influences. Questionable ethics, drugs, and sexual license are prevalent in today's society.
   C. We must take our stand for Christ even if it means ridicule and persecution. Christ will furnish the needed strength and courage, and give assurance of divine approval. Mark 8:38